ON THE PRODUCTION OF KNOWLEDGE

COMPARATIVE ASIAN STUDIES

Editors: Frans Hüsken and Dick Kooiman
Assistant executive editor: José Komen, Centre for Asian Studies Amsterdam

Publications in this series:
1. CONCEPTUALIZING DEVELOPMENT: The Historical-Sociological Tradition in Dutch Non-Western Sociology / Otto van den Muyzenberg and Willem Wolters / isbn 90-6765-382-9 39 pages ppb.
2. THE SHATTERED IMAGE: Construction and Deconstruction of the Village in Colonial Asia / Jan Breman / isbn 90-6765-383-7 50 pages ppb.
3. SEDUCTIVE MIRAGE: The Search for the Village Community in Southeast Asia / Jeremy Kemp / isbn 90-6765-384-5 47 pages ppb.
4. BETWEEN SOVEREIGN DOMAIN AND SERVILE TENURE: The Development of Rights to Land in Java, 1780-1870 / Peter Boomgaard / isbn 90-6256-788-6 61 pages ppb.
5. LABOUR MIGRATION AND RURAL TRANSFORMATION IN COLONIAL ASIA / Jan Breman / isbn 90-6256-873-4 82 pages ppb.
6. LIVING IN DELI: Its Society as Imaged in Colonial Fiction / Lily E. Clerkx and Wim F. Wertheim / isbn 90-6256-965-X 126 pages ppb.
7. STATE, VILLAGE, AND RITUAL IN BALI: A Historical Perspective / Henk Schulte Nordholt / isbn 90-5383-023-5 58 pages ppb.
8. THE CENTRALITY OF CENTRAL ASIA / Andre Gunder Frank / isbn 90-5383-079-0 68 pages ppb.
9. IDEOLOGICAL INNOVATION UNDER MONARCHY: Aspects of Legitimation Activity in Contemporary Brunei / G. Graighlinn / isbn 90-5383-091-X 112 pages ppb.
10. THE STATE OF BIHAR / Arvind N. Das / isbn 90-5383-135-5 116 pages ppb.
11. ON THE PRODUCTION OF KNOWLEDGE: Fieldwork in South Gujarat, 1971-1991 / Hein Streefkerk / isbn 90-5383-188-6 56 pages ppb.

CENTRE FOR ASIAN STUDIES AMSTERDAM

Hein Streefkerk

On the Production of Knowledge

Fieldwork in South Gujarat, 1971-1991

VU University Press
Amsterdam, 1993

VU University Press is an imprint of:
VU Boekhandel/Uitgeverij bv
De Boelelaan 1105
1081 HV Amsterdam
The Netherlands

Editing by: V. Crawford, Volcano
Lay-out by: Sjoukje Rienks, Amsterdam
Printed by: Haveka bv, Alblasserdam

ISBN   90-5383-188-6
NUGI   653

Contents

1. *Looking Back*

This publication consists of three methodological reflections. The first two were originally published in Dutch in 1972 and 1977; I wrote the third a short time ago. They are based on research conducted among the workers and owners of small industrial enterprises[1] in South Gujarat, on the west coast of India.[2]

There are several reasons for translating and republishing these articles together. They share a common location and theme, and give the reader a look behind the scenes at fieldwork, something which was unusual in those days. Further, the articles are instructive for a younger generation of field-workers since they consider topics which are still current, such as the manipulation of informants and the improvisational nature of fieldwork. However, I finally decided to republish the articles after hearing the reaction to the first article by a much younger Indian colleague who had just carried out fieldwork in Amsterdam. He was surprised at my ethical deliberations in the 1970s. I realised that he was really reacting to the intellectual climate of the early seventies among sociologists and anthropologists in Amsterdam and elsewhere in Western Europe and the United States. The first two articles thus provide insight into the discussions of the early seventies, and in doing so they form part of the recent history of the social sciences. This is closely related to the theme of the third article, which I happened to be writing at that time. In that paper I discuss how I perceived the industrial developments in South Gujarat, which I had studied in the seventies, in 1990.

During the last two decades the ideological and theoretical backgrounds of the various social sciences have changed continually. For example, struc-tural-functionalism and the evolutionary approach to modernisation, which were dominant until the late sixties, have declined in importance. Interactionism flourished in social anthropology, the 'world-system' approach became important and the 'political economy of growth' came to dominate the anthropology and sociology of 'development'. During the 1980s the latter approach lost its prominence and gave way to the study of cultural and ideological dimensions of domination and subordination. During the same period, feminism achieved a central position within sociology and anthropology. Finally, anthropological fieldwork was de-mythologised. It will be obvious that these developments were related.

1

From the mid-1960s, and particularly around 1970, the function, relevance and credibility of the social sciences were increasingly questioned.[3] The 'concerned scholar' who wanted to do more than just study racial prejudices, social inequality or repression (Köbben 1972), who showed concern about the possible unintended use of his or her research results, and who was critical of the dominant ideology and its social consequences, became a leading ideal for many.

The discussion about the meaning and use of social science research was accompanied by increased openness about the way fieldwork was actually carried out. In this connection, the question of the acceptability of the researcher's activities was often raised. This problem, together with the discussion of the meaning and uses of research, raised so many ethical questions that there was an explosive increase in the number of publications on ethics-related topics (Kloos 1972, Van Olden 1972).[4] In the Netherlands, colleagues at the Anthropological-Sociological Centre of the University of Amsterdam began planning a conference, 'The ethics of social science research, in particular with regard to the Third World'. This took place in 1972 and was organised by the Netherlands Association of Sociology and Anthropology. The first article in this publication was written for that conference. It is about the ethics of fieldwork and, more important, it gives a 'backstage' view of fieldwork. I wrote it shortly after my return from South Gujarat, at a time when I was still very concerned about my often deceptive research behaviour, while at the same time realising that some informants had used me equally for their own purposes. These were topics which I had not yet encountered in the literature. At the time some colleagues still thought that "those were things you shouldn't write about", as such topics were not considered essential in the production of knowledge.[5] In later years, however, this 'backstage' became increasingly public.[6] For example, in 1978 a book entitled *Achter de Coulissen* ('Behind the Scenes') appeared in Dutch. It was about fieldwork in Ghana, though the author published it under the pseudonym of 'Wolf Bleek'.

The necessarily improvised nature of fieldwork, and particularly the problems which arise when it is carried out under circumstances which are characterised by fundamental contradictions between dominant and subordinate groups (which is the topic of my second paper) was another subject which did not receive much attention at the time. Here it was also the case that researchers did not give much publicity to how they really did their fieldwork, nor to their inability to heed methodological prescriptions in practice. Reports on these topics, and on the role of contingency and luck in successful fieldwork, did not fit into the dominant ideal of how social science research was supposed to be done. The discipline was still overburdened by its attempts to be accepted as scientific, in the sense of the positivistic natural science ideal. The maintenance of a strict methodological format, counting and measuring, and statistical manipulation were therefore independent and praiseworthy activities (Brunt 1977: 8, 9).

The discussion about the meaning and use of social science research and the rising ideal of the 'concerned scholar' also led to a wider recognition of qualitative methods. Positivism became a synonym for a conservative and ahistorical form of scientific practice. Such positivism served mainly to verify the researcher's ideas and offered insufficient possibilities for the reconstruction of the ideas and situation of those studied. Moreover, researchers became more aware of the unavoidable unreliability of much quantitative material and its inability to provide an adequate picture of complex reality.

These problems which have been raised since the late 1960s can also be interpreted as a debate about the bias or neutrality of the fieldworker, about involvement or detachment, and about reality as a creation of the researcher or as an independent entity; in short, about the subjectivity and objectivity of sociology and anthropology.

Twenty years after Scholte (1972: 431, 439) wrote that anthropological activity is never only 'scientific' and that "cultural contexts and personal circumstances precede ethnographic description as such and affect empirical data gathered", the discussion about the subjectivity and objectivity of the social sciences, or at least of cultural anthropology and ethnography, appears to have been decided in favour of the subjective approach.[7] Kloos (1987: 31) proceeds from a dialectical approach to anthropological knowledge, which he sees as being created in the interaction between the fieldworker and his or her socio-cultural background on the one hand, and the people whose way of life he or she studies on the other. Clifford (1990: 2, 7) is of the opinion that ethnography "always [has been] caught up in the invention, not the representation, of cultures", and that "ethnographic truths are thus inherently partial - committed and incomplete."

This perspective is not new. For a long time anthropologists have been aware of their role in the construction of others' cultures and ways of life. Thus it is all the more striking that positivistic ideals relating to the nature of knowledge still dominate the presentation of anthropologists' research results, and that the background of their insights has no place in their monographs (Kloos 1987: 35). Herd and Stoller (1990: 6, 25) express surprise about this as well. In spite of the recognition that 'subjectivity edits observation', the ethnographer's personal experiences, which form the background of his or her data, are absent in the text which he or she finally produces. They also point to the apparently still dominant positivistic ideal of objectivity, which leads to the exclusion of this information from the final reports. Yet learning a culture is a subjective activity. The representation of another people's way of life rests on the researcher's own interpretations, which are then ordered and recorded in accordance with his or her frame of reference.

The unavoidable question which arises is whether the problem of subjectivity is perhaps less cogent when the object of study is more concrete, more 'factual'. This seems to be the case, for example, in the case of fieldwork on the way in which nature, labour and capital are exploited. The variables and indicators are, after all, easier to observe, quantifiable and often already available in the form of secondary material. In other words, the positivistic ideal of science appears to be more easily realisible when the goal of fieldwork is to find out who controls land, labour and their products, the nature of the available technology, the volume and composition of capital invested, the character of industrial production, the social background of entrepreneurs and how they behave, the origin of the workers, how much they earn and under what circumstances, their relationships to their superiors and to each other, the role of the state, etc. This is supported by four of the five dissertations which have been written at the University of Amsterdam during the last few years, which were based on fieldwork in Asia and covered the above-mentioned topics (Hüsken 1988, Van Wersch 1989, Rutten 1990, Rutten 1991).[8] The fieldwork and the reporting appear to have been carried out unproblematically according to the principles of objectivity, distance and neutrality.[9] The fifth dissertation (Nieuwenhuys 1990), however, shows that the object of study does not determine the degree of objectivity in research itself or in writing about it. Nieuwenhuys investigated children's labour in Kerala, and she writes that her book is a subjective product, in spite of her attempts "at elucidating the material and economic conditions in which children's work is set" (1990: 23). Her own experience as a child who worked formed, not always consciously, the driving force behind her interest in working children in India. This personal experience, together with quantitative data and 'in-depth anthropological methods' made it possible for her "to shed some light on the world of those who have been left in the dark too often" (1990: xv, xix). The same view is evident in Breman's (1985a) earlier study. He describes extensively his own bias during fieldwork among sugar cane cutters, on the way in which "sugar cane and labour are crushed in the sugar factories in West India" (Breman 1985b). His involvement enabled him to observe a reality which would otherwise have remained invisible. Ideological orientation and engagement were an integral part of his role as a fieldworker. Fieldwork probably facilitated Breman's expression of his preferences. His work, indeed, shows that it is not the nature of the object of study which determines the influence of the fieldworker's perception on the collection and reporting of data.

The subjective character of the reality which the fieldworker presents demands that he or she enables the reader to judge the acceptability of his or her reconstruction. Following Kloos (1987: 46, 48) and Herd and Stoller (1990: 28), this requires that the assumptions and personal background which have contributed to the knowledge presented are made explicit. This is not only important for evaluating the credibility of knowledge at a given moment, but also necessary for interpreting continuing research. It is obvious that in order to judge the results of a later study, carried out by a different researcher, the assumptions of both researchers should be known. This approach is also a must when the second study is carried out by the same fieldworker, as the immutability of a researcher's frame of reference should not be taken for granted. This is the topic of the third article, in which I discuss, among other things, whether the things which struck me in Bulsar in 1990, almost 20 years after my first visit, were the result of a different reality, a different frame of reference, or a combination of both.

2. *On Participation and Manipulation*

The ethical problems which confront the fieldworker in the Third World can be categorised as follows: 1) problems that relate to the goal and utility of the research, and 2) problems which arise from the fieldwork situation itself. One could argue that if the goals and utility of the research are considered legitimate, the researcher's fieldwork procedures need not be questioned. Even if this is the case, however, it does not mean that the researcher's concrete problems disappear automatically. To illustrate this, I will discuss the manipulation of informants. The topic is examined in the context of a particular research technique: fieldwork based on loosely structured interviews conducted during repeated visits. This does not imply that participant observation, the other major fieldwork technique, precludes the manipulation of informants. However, the problem is urgent now because the loosely structured interview highlights it rather sharply, and because fieldworkers increasingly employ this technique. Furthermore, the social context, of which the researcher himself is a part, is changing. And finally, researchers have increasingly come to doubt their goals and methods in sociological and anthropological research.

In the anthropological literature, ethical problems are usually dealt with in terms of role-conflict. The shortcomings of this mode of explanation will be dealt with in the following pages.

The experiences and opinions presented here are based on research on small-scale industries in South Gujarat, India, carried out between April 1971 and February 1972 in the small town of Bulsar and its surroundings. The town, which had about 50,000 inhabitants in 1971, is located at about 200 kilometers north of Bombay.

Modes of Data Collection

In order to discuss the problem, it is necessary to look at the way I collected my data. I defined an industrial entrepreneur as someone who produces outside his home; i.e., in a workshop with the help of non-animal energy and more or less complex machinery, and who employs at least a few paid workers. The definition excluded the owners of the so-called 'cottage industries', since their inclusion would have made the category of 'small-scale industry' too large and heterogeneous. Moreover, my interest was principally in industries which used modern techniques, which demanded more than a nominal financial investment to set up, and which enjoyed considerable financial and administrative support from the government. There was no serious problem of confusing small-scale industry with medium- and large-scale industries, since the latter were virtually non-existent. The only exception was a huge chemical complex set up with foreign investment.

It was by applying the above criteria that a sample of 55 entrepreneurs was arrived at from a universe of 220. This sample constituted the core informants. However, owners of enterprises outside the sample also served as informants when it seemed that they could provide useful information.

The method of participant observation did not lend itself well to this research, since the majority of informants were not located in one area of Bulsar, but were spread out over the entire town. A few lived on the outskirts of town or outside it, while some spent a major part of the week in Bombay. The factories also were not concentrated in one area. Some were located within the town, others along the approach roads to Bulsar, while yet others were to be found in an industrial area which lay about 3 kilometers from the town.

Further, it was not sufficient to approach entrepreneurs on the basis of their membership in manufacturers' associations since only some of them were organised in this manner. In any case, the associations did not appear to be particularly active.

My research questions were such that I had to collect information which varied from family history to business practices, including the evasion of labour laws and bribing of officials. Clearly, such sensitive subjects could not be approached through bland survey techniques. Consequently, I had to adopt a strategy which could neither be based on participant observation nor on survey techniques. This was the loosely-structured interview, which involved repeatedly visiting the same informant, either at home or in the factory. With some entrepreneurs, it became possible to build up more or less lasting relationships. The information sought from them was solicited during the course of extensive talks.

Participant versus Interviewer

This mode of conducting research differs from that of 'traditional' anthropology, where research sought to study 'the entire culture and social life' (Evans-Pritchard 1964: 77). The difference arises from the growing problem-orientedness of current research; this research focuses on specific parts of the 'entire culture and social life'. Furthermore, research is conducted in

7

communities which are no longer - and probably have never been - 'closed' in Evans-Pritchard's sense. And, finally, the position of the contemporary researcher per se is also different from that of cultural anthropologists in the past. Barnes (1967: 195) refers to this change in terms of 'colonial and post-colonial conditions'. He observes that in the past the subjects of research were brought under a microscope and that the researchers were, as it were, 'looking down the tube at them'. Even Malinowski saw his Trobriand informants as specimens in laboratory research. It was a period where "superior knowledge in practical matters, such as medicine and influence with the dominant political group [...] may contribute towards creating for him the privileged position of a special friend and helper in need" (Nadel 1939: 326). Such a superior position is hardly as evident for researchers now. The group or institution which is the subject of research is seen in the context of a network of social relationships, of which the researcher is an integral or reluctant constituent (Barnes 1967: 179). The researcher must recognise that the informant is a person to be reckoned with; indeed, this is virtually dictated by necessity if the researcher wants to succeed in realising his research goals. For instance, it often happened in Bulsar that factory owners got irritated after a while and took the initiative to terminate conversations; some did not even allow me to enter their buildings. All this seems to be quite far from Evans-Pritchard's remark that "an anthropologist has failed unless, when he says good-bye to the natives, there is on both sides the sorrow of parting" (1964: 79). The docile native of yesteryear is capable of positing himself, and of asking questions like: "So you're doing a little research; tell me why and what you've found."

It is my impression that discussions about the role of the researcher and ethical questions have not kept in step with the changes in the position of the researcher as described above. There is a tendency to extrapolate from opinions of a past period in order to examine contemporary problems. The ideal of neutrality of the researcher is one of these older ideas. It is recommended by Evans-Prichard (1964: 79) and, for example, by Barnes (1967: 203), when he speaks of 'ethical problems in modern fieldwork', though he recognizes that its realization sometimes is problematical. The desirability of a neutral position certainly arises from the privileged position of the researcher a few decades ago.

Extrapolation of this position also has consequences in the way the question of ethical integrity is dealt with, as it is typically conceived as being one of conflicting values. The honest anthropologist finds himself in a bind between the values of his informants and those prevailing in his own society. Jarvie (1969) advises the anthropologist to choose the values of his own society in such circumstances. This solution suggests the idea of freedom of choice which inheres in the fieldworker's belief in his neutrality.

As long as the fieldworker is able to maintain this belief Jarvie's advice might be of some help, but it is of little use in solving ethical questions which arise during the process of collecting information, as I will explain later on. Of particular importance are the problems which arise from the necessity of entering into relationships with informants in order to elicit information. The permanent presence and face-to-face contacts of anthropologists engaging in participant observation and the casual nature of the data collecting could explain the lack of attention to this subject.

The difference in the mode of work of the 'traditional' fieldworker and one where the accent is on repeated visits and loosely structured interviews is in the interrupted, discontinuous character of the interview procedure. In contrast to participation in relatively 'closed' communities, where the informant is engaged in social interaction with his informants on an almost daily basis and, for example, friendships can form spontaneously, the interview situation is one where only limited contacts are possible and spontaneity is often reduced to the minimum. The pressure on the researcher to collect as much information as possible within these constraints is, consequently, greater than the similar pressure facing the participant observer. The resources which the interviewer can bring to bear on this situation and the ethical problems inherent to it are discussed below.

Role Conflict?

One of the first enterprises I visited was located in the centre of Bulsar town. It consisted of several small factories manufacturing synthetic cloth, fiber-glass helmets and plastic buckets. A small chemical plant was under construction. It is, like most small industrial enterprises, a family-owned company.

On my first visit, I was given to understand by a younger brother that his elder brother had gone to Delhi. He said that he would prefer to withhold discussion until his elder brother returned. I was luckier the second time around. The elder brother, Nanubhai, was willing to talk to me and the conversation was satisfactory. The atmosphere was formal and there was an - entirely unnecessary - interpreter present; yet I came away with the impression that the elder brother would make a good informant who would reveal more in a more intimate setting. Therefore, I decided to make some 'work' out of him. I followed up this meeting with more visits, and he invited me to dinner at his home. The relationship became more friendly, especially from his side. One of the consequences of this was that it led to lengthy conversations. He told me, for example, about the problems of joint-family life. During another meeting, he spoke at length about the corrupt practices of officials, as well as his own. At the conclusion of these encounters, I found myself in a state of emotional confusion, which I was unable to address. Moreover, I realised later that I had difficulties in remembering parts of our conversations.

With Desai, a manufacturer of chemicals, the element of friendship was not so marked; yet there was certainly an element of trust. Under cover of the fact that I was a foreigner - he said so in so many words - he gave me information concerning bribery, with the specific instruction that I was not to commit what he said to paper. My reaction was to let my notebook remain in my bag; on reaching home, however, I immediately wrote notes on everything that he had said. This encounter occurred later than that with Nanubhai. By this time I had discovered my tendency not to listen when subjects were raised and things were told which I was supposed not to 'hear', and I then knew that I had to force myself to 'store' the information.

The emotional confusion which I experienced at the initial stage of my fieldwork and the habit of listening with only half an ear, combined with the tendency to repress what I had learned, can be clarified by using the concept of role-conflict. The conflict between the roles of friend and researcher led to psychological discomfort and a tendency to repress confidential information: one can hear various things as a friend, but not as a researcher. Later on, after becoming aware of my reactions, I tried to be a researcher first. This indeed enabled me to be more attentive, but it did not solve the ethical dilemmas which I experienced more clearly from then onwards, like noting down information which the informant had clearly said should not be put to paper.

Jarvie (1969) maintains that the crises of ethical integrity and identity of the anthropologist can be resolved "by allowing one role to override the other", and that "the anthropologist must choose the role of a stranger, because only that role allows him to act in what he and the society he comes from would consider to be his integrity as a member of that society in general and as a scientist in particular." Kloos (1969), who also clarifies fieldwork problems in terms of conflicting roles, disagrees with Jarvie. According to Kloos, "the problem of role conflict during fieldwork is partly insoluble." Though they draw different conclusions, both authors cite similar situations in order to make their arguments. For them, the context is provided by intensive participant observation with their objects within earshot. My impression is that for them the twin statuses of insider-outsider, friend-stranger, etc., are most pressing and the dilemma concerning standards of behaviour is most acute during dramatic events, such as illnesses, quarrels, lynchings, and so on. This is in contrast to my experience, where I did not meet my informants daily and I was not involved in such dramatic incidents. Nevertheless, I felt uneasiness almost continuously during my fieldwork.

Manipulation

The contradiction between the roles of friend and researcher indeed throws some light on my psychological discomfort. However, it is not a conclusive explanation for the tension I felt during my fieldwork. Often the role of friend did not come easily to me and did not really interfere with my researcher role since I hardly felt any friendship. Thus my uneasiness cannot be attributed to conflict between the roles of friend and researcher alone.

Instead, its origin lay in what I would call the hypocrisy of the whole procedure. Role conflict could be seen as a possible cause in the sense that the expectations of the informant were not in consonance with how I had constructed my role as a researcher. A certain degree of friendship was suggested and a certain amount of reciprocity was assumed, although such reciprocity did not exist. In other words, the reciprocity was given differing values by the parties concerned: for the informant, it was an affective relationship, while for me it was ultimately an instrumental one. The issue is not the conflict between two roles, but the fieldworker's manipulation - in a refined manner - of informants by performing different roles and moving consciously from one role to the other, from friend to researcher.

Jarvie (1969: 505-507) recognizes this procedure: "... to some extent the success of the method of participant observation derives from exploiting the situation created by role clashes (of) insider/outsider, stranger/friend, pupil/teacher [...] moreover fragments of evidence exist which suggest that in the field situation conscious use may have to be made of the 'stranger' position by the stranger in order to elicit information."

My research strategy consisted of playing out various possibilities which presented themselves. In the introductory phase, the fact of being a foreigner was emphasised, since I then could take advantage of Indian hospitality. By doing so, I was invited home, food was served and the ice was broken. I continued to use the status of innocent foreigner when it suited my purposes to do so. Otherwise, relationships were given a connotation of friendship, provided the behaviour of the informant gave an indication as to whether he was open to a friendly relationship or not. Spontaneous feelings of friendship, though of an ambivalent nature, did occur. However, they were the result of what was, in the first instance, constructed as an instrumental relationship. As soon as the relationship had become more affective, the tension between the roles of friend and researcher began to mount. This uneasiness is in fact secondary to the ethical and moral question of my manipulative strategy.

Sometimes informants became suspicious when they came to know that I had also built up good relationships with others. My reaction was to suggest to the concerned informant that my relationships with others were more businesslike, while that with him was more personal.

One might conclude that the relationship between researcher and informant is an unequal one, that the latter must suffer the refined 'tricks' of the former. It would mean that anthropological research is less egalitarian than is sometimes supposed (Brunt-de Wit 1972: 46). This observation is not wholly true. The researcher is also the subject of manipulation, as the following example illustrates.

I spent a fortnight with an informant about 30 kilometers from my own residence. He was an amiable man who did all that he could to ensure that I was comfortable. I was seen as a family member, and suffered all the attendant disadvantages of this status. I felt hampered in my research, since I was not free to meet people without his prior approval. I was used as a status object, taken to marriages and had to make appearances in front of other members of the family and his friends. On one occasion, I was urged to go along on a visit to my host's 'best friend' on the grounds that he had looked forward to meeting me for a long time. When we reached the friend's home, another visitor was already present; it was obvious that my host was aware of this. The visitor turned out to be a powerful and important man; we sat for hours, consumed alcohol in immoderate quantities, and the three men engaged in heated discussion. At one point, my host broke off the discussion on the grounds that we had to return home since I was tired. It transpired that the visitor wanted my host to do something for him, but my host was unwilling to concede the favour. Since he had known in advance that such a favour would be asked of him, he had taken me along in order to provide a valid excuse to cover his departure and to postpone having to make a decision. This example shows that I had no choice which role I could play. I had to act as the 'pleasant guest', the 'adopted son', or a 'tired foreigner'.

I have tried to show how the researcher manipulates his informants and how the informants use the researcher to suit their own purposes. I agree with Lundberg (1968) who is of the opinion that the researcher-informant relationship must be described in a dynamic way. The depiction of the relationship in terms of 'exchange', in which a certain amount of reciprocity is taken for granted, is certainly useful and points to the egalitarian aspects of this relationship. The researcher gets his information and the informant receives 'some sort of psychological gratification' by way of 'confirmation', the opportunity to express one's opinions and stances without fear of rebuttal. But Lundberg also maintains that 'the relationship between informant and researcher is purposefully differentiated since it is the primary activity for the researcher and usually the secondary activity for the informant. For what he receives the researcher may not be able to offer much tangibly in the way of return since he typically is limited in financial resources or anything else the informant consciously wants directly'.

Lundberg's opinion does not differ much from my ideas. I believe that the relationship between informant and researcher is largely determined by the fieldworker. He initiates the relation by exploiting the opportunities offered by roles such as foreigner, visitor, etc., in order to build up a relationship which is meant to be instrumental in the first place. During the period of the relationship, the researcher manipulates the informant, through affection and emotion, to glean as much information as possible within the limited time available to him. I agree that providing information can imply psychological statisfaction for the informant, but the gratification is not of the same order or importance as the information gathered by the researcher. However, informants should not be seen as being entirely powerless or inarticulate, since they can withhold information and bring their own resources to bear on the situation and, indeed, use the researcher for their own purposes.

Brymer and Farris (1967: 305) take up the issue of the manipulation of informants more empathically. They are informed by Goffman's 'Presentation of Self in Everyday Life' and see "variations among actors (researchers) in the degree to which they can manipulate an audience (respondents), and among audiences in the degree to which they can withstand, or 'see through' the actor's presentation ... [T]ime and time again it has been observed that respondents tend to give information more easily to the researcher who appears to be a 'good guy' [...] For sociologists, the ethical problem is whether the researcher has the right to use information given to him by a lower-class person - or any person, for that matter - under the assumption that the researcher is a 'good guy', even where the researcher has made his identity known." The authors do not offer a solution to this dilemma. They point to it in order to show that the problem is beyond the researcher's control, and that it is impossible to resolve it in advance.

It is significant that their greatest worry seems to be with whether or not the researcher should use the information which he collected in his guise as a 'good guy', while to me the manner in which the information was collected should have been of primary concern. At the end of their article (314, 315), they state, "In moral-ethical terms, we have come to the conclusion that one needs an ethic which transcends the groups, persons or situations involved in the ethical issue. We have come to view 'ethical' problems as the result of the collision of groups or persons having different interests [...]

actually what we have developed is not so much a set of ethical precepts as a set of ethical procedures ... [F]irst, one should seek a commonality of interests which transcends the parties involved as well as the immediate situation in which the collision of interests occurs. There is an assumption that these sorts of common interests can be found, or created, among all human groups" (314-315). This recommendation is attractive because is practical, though it does not provide any protection for informants.

Some of my fieldwork among entrepreneurs was aimed at finding out how they dealt with officials and 'rules and regulations', topics about which they were reluctant to talk. So when I wanted to raise the subject, I pretended to know more than I did about the inefficiency of the government machinery, and about its causes, how they felt about it, and how they coped with it. Because the malfunctioning of administration was a popular subject, entrepreneurs were eager to talk about it. Perhaps they even believed that I would be able to do something about it on their behalf. At any rate, I collected information during these conversations which I probably would never have come across otherwise. It is rather easy for the researcher to find a common interest, but whether this interest is really 'common' is open to doubt.

Conclusion

Anthropological and sociological fieldwork implies manipulation of informants. This is more pronounced when, unlike participant observation, contacts between fieldworkers and informants are fleeting and research is based on visits and loosely structured interviews. Limited access to informants forces the fieldworker to play different roles in order to establish relations and to elicit information. The use of these techniques is not restricted to research in non-Western areas, but I believe that non-Western settings offer an 'easier' terrain for the collection of information in this manner than one's own society. Non-Western societies provide more and easier opportunities to adopt different roles through which information can be collected. For example, in India, the fieldworker can play the roles of ignorant stranger, guest or friend. Furthermore, he can use the possibilities offered by a society based on hierarchy.

If the ethics of the research strategy are debatable, and they often are, then one can raise the question of its justification. The ultimate legitimation of techniques lies with the research itself; i.e., the goals it seeks to fulfill. The purposes can vary considerably, from a wish to accumulate scientific knowledge, to an intention to let the people studied benefit from its results, to a need to have something published.

14

The framing of an ethical code to spell out the norms governing this kind of research seems to be an impossible exercise, unless one is prepared to forbid some types of research altogether, not only in anthropology and sociology, but also in related disciplines.

3. *Through the Back Door*

Many publications based on anthropological or sociological fieldwork give the impression that the researcher knew from the outset what he wanted to investigate and how he was going to go about it. Further, there seemed to be no problems with the realization of these goals. The preface of such research typically thanks institutions, key informants and other respondents for their unstinting cooperation. If a survey formed part of the research plan, the sample seemed to have been impeccably selected and invariably brought new and interesting data to light. As far as in-depth, qualitative data was concerned, the researcher was fortunate to have befriended the right persons. Of course, the circumstances under which the research was conducted were far from ideal; the researcher was far from home, it was hot and the work was often strenuous. Fortunately, such problems were overcome with the help of an understanding spouse or partner, who is invariably warmly thanked in the preface.

Such publications, which radiate an aura of expertise and success, tend to be more disheartening than stimulating for the reader who is contemplating doing fieldwork for the first time. The author's level of perfection seems difficult to match. It was only after I had done fieldwork myself and had talked to other fieldworkers that I came to realise that such publications do not give a true picture of what really happened. Instead, the accounts are often tailored to be in accordance with scientific ideals and norms such as objectivity, reliability and systematic thought. The underlying assumption is that it is possible for the fieldworker to grasp 'reality' as an independent researcher with the help of certain research techniques. That the actual process of conducting research often entails that reality influences both the researcher as well as the course of his research is almost never referred to. Research which fails is seldom considered worthy of publication and such reports are therefore unlikely to come to the reader's attention. Further, the researcher who does succeed has a vested interest in withholding information which would compromise his data and methods. After all, he has to keep his financiers and project sponsors happy, and for them, 'hard' results are most important. The scientific community and his promotor are also on the lookout for evidence of scientific competence.

In this essay I will discuss the little freedom and limited autonomy of the fieldworker. The basis for the discussion is my research among owners of small industrial enterprises and their workers. I sought, in part, to enquire after the nature and size of small-scale industrial developments, with particular reference to working conditions and labour relations. I had to collect both qualitative as well as quantitative data. The difficult accessibility of my field of study, however, meant that the process of data-collection was far less systematic than I had hoped.

First, I will examine the reasons for the unreliability of existing data and explain the selective and guarded disclosure of information on the part of my informants. In order to do so I must clarify the relations between the government officials, entrepreneurs, and workers which set the stage for my research. Then I will describe how I tried to stand up to these problems and will discuss the quality of the data which I collected. In the conclusion, I will discuss the significance of the problems I encountered for the implementation of development policy in general, since such policy is typically targeted at the poorest among the local population.

Incomplete Lists and Suspicious Owners

A study of industrial development necessitates the collection of statistics about the number of companies and the number of workers employed by them. A first orientation made it clear that the information contained in official documents was incomplete as well as unreliable. One example was the collection of lists maintained by the industries officer. This functionary was responsible for supervision of local industry amd for maintenance of records concerning the number of industrial units and the number of workers employed in them. These lists also contained such data as the level of investment, the end product, turnover and the number of workers. However, only registered firms were listed, and many enterprises did not figure in the listings at all. Further, some listed firms had shut down, while others appeared never to have existed. This incompleteness was partly clarified by the absence of a compulsory registration procedure for small-scale industries. Only those undertakings which made use of services and facilities provided by government agencies were obliged to register. Some entrepreneurs who wished to profit from the services offered set up companies which existed only on paper. The facilities thus obtained were channeled for other ends. For example, the possession of import licenses for scarce raw materials and certain machines allowed these entrepreneurs to sel! off the imported goods in the black market at a handsome profit.

It was also clear from the outset that to determine the number of industrial units and the number of employed in these enterprises, I had to do the counting myself:

In the very beginning my assistant, an inhabitant of Bulsar, tried to enumerate the workers. He would regularly return with empty hands, since the owners had refused to disclose information or had said that they would only talk to me. Moreover, it appeared that the information that he received was suspiciously similar. If the owners were to be believed, they did not employ more than ten workers. When I asked them how many workers they employed, they often gave the same answer. In some cases, this was true, but in most cases, this figure had no relation to reality. A quick look around the shop-floor was enough to conclude that there were more employees than the owner would have liked me to believe.

It quickly transpired that it was in the entrepreneurs' interest to show as few workers as possible, since this resulted in a significant savings in labour costs. These savings arose from the fact that labour laws came into operation only when the number of workers was more than ten. The labour laws set standards of hygiene and safety on the shop floor, made provision for paid leave and the sharing of profits between owner and labour, and forbade child labour. Further conditions were imposed when the number of workers rose to more than fifty: the owners were then obliged to contribute towards a pension fund for the workers.

The owners were able to disguise the true number of workers in their enterprises since the government officers who were vested with the responsibility for control exercised their powers on a limited scale, and that to the advantage of the owners. Their loyalties were with the owners rather than with the workers, with the result that the owners got away with double bookkeeping, the sanitized version being reserved for government officials. Another way of getting around the labour laws was to split the business into smaller administrative units which would exist only on paper, and which invariably had less than 10 or 50 workers.

This splitting up serves more than one purpose. It allows for a lowering of taxable income and enables owners to employ workers on a temporary basis by transferring them from one company to the other. Further, entrepreneurs can make more extensive use of government facilities, since two separate companies can claim more facilities than one. It was, therefore, not easy to build up an accurate quantitative picture of the number of small-scale industries in the research area. It is even more difficult to sketch developments over a period of time in quantitative terms. Furthermore, it is certain that the official sources give an exaggerated idea of the total number of small-scale industries.

Many entrepreneurs did not like my efforts to count the number of workers, and they gave incomplete information and tried to hinder my attempts to visit the shop floor. This was not only due to their wish to disguise the number of workers, but also showed their reluctance to reveal working conditions. The prospect of an outsider's gaining insight into these conditions, which often were appalling and certainly did not conform to official rules, was just as intimidating to the owners' peace of mind.

In one of the small plastic factories outside Bulsar there were only a few workers present during my visit. The owner was absent; the accountant had been left in charge. I was allowed to take a look at the shop floor. The picture was far from elevating. A few children, not more than 12 or 13 years of age, sat on top of the plastic injectors in a badly ventilated space, feeding the raw material into the machine. They were made to work for 12 hours a day. After some time the owner, warned by the accountant, angrily arrived at the workshop, forced me to go outside and made it clear that my presence was not wanted.

The implicit threat which my presence seemed to imply would probably have been less if the firms had not been hit eighteen months earlier by actions for better wages and working conditions. By reacting harshly, owners successfully resisted the actions; most of the strikes failed. Since then the entrepreneurs tried to prevent anything which threatened to disturb the status quo.[10] My interest in workers and their conditions was seen as a possible source of disruption.

As the following paragraphs will show, owners were not the only source for data on the number of workers. However, I was entirely dependent on them when it came to such matters as the economic viability of the enterprise and its financial achievements. My curiosity in this area was as unwelcome to the entrepreneurs as my interest in the workers. Consequently, I was forced to give up my plan of collecting 'hard' figures about these topics.

> The owners were not prepared to give accurate data on the financial position of their enterprises. This reticence could be attributed to the fact that they were either evading some taxes or misusing facilities and services provided by the government, or both. At the most, some of them were willing to talk about their monthly turnover. But they consciously under-reported its volume, since this allowed them to not pay a bonus to the workers. Further, a low turnover also gave an excuse to plead for postponement of debt repayments.

In a Roundabout Way

In order to cope with the problem of the reluctant owner, I entered their sheds by the back doors, through the shop floors, counting the number of workers as I made my way to the office. Exact figures could not be arrived at in this way, especially when the number of workers was quite large.

Another possibility was to ask the workers how many colleagues they had. This method was not satisfactory either, because their estimates were also seldom accurate, especially when they worked for a larger company. Furthermore, they did not represent all industrial units located in the research area. Yet I was able to arrive at approximate figures by combining the different possibilities. In my estimation, the number of workers in the entire research area could be put at 2500 without doing too much violence to reality. The official figures were markedly lower. The Employment Exchange, the second official source of information, counted 1320 workers during a voluntary census held about a year before.

However, I was unable to go much further than a synchronic picture. On the basis of information about the date of establishment of the enterprises in Bulsar and conversations with well-informed inhabitants of the town, I reached the obvious conclusion that the number of undertakings and workers had shown a marked increase in the last 10 to 15 years. It was not possible to chart the fluctuations in this development over a period of time. The inaccuracy of the data available to me made it difficult to suggest relationships between, for example, the increase in the number of industrial workers and the demographic changes which had occurred in the sub-district. These drawbacks did not allow for more than a superficial quantitative evaluation of the policy with reference to small-scale industries in general and the creation of non-agrarian employment in particular.

The investigation of working conditions and labour relations had to proceed with caution due to the recent tensions between owners and workers, and the vulnerable position of the latter. I was obliged to be on good terms with the owners since I wanted to know what they thought about their workers and how they tried to keep them under control. At the same time, however, I was also anxious to maintain a relationship of trust with the workers. Therefore, I had to try to ensure that the workers who cooperated with me did not run into trouble with their employers. If I had been able to conduct two separate yet concomitant pieces of research, I would have been able to overcome problems generated by my simultaneous interest in both owners and workers. Such a design, however, could not be realised in a research area which consisted of a small town and its immediate environment. I was quickly recognised in public, my neighbours became friends, and among their friends were owners of industrial enterprises. In the long run it was difficult to continue to disguise my intentions. The workers realised that I regularly visited the owners, and the owners in turn knew that I was not averse to talking to the workers.

Nevertheless, I tried initially to meet the workers outside the factories, far from the eyes of the owners. In this way, I hoped to hide my interests from the owners, to protect the workers and to create an opportunity for them to speak freely. I traced workers according to the 'snowball' method: I started with a few workers whom I happened to know, and they introduced me to their relatives and colleagues. The advantage of this technique was that the new informant was inclined to trust me, since the introduction had occurred through someone he knew. The disadvantage, however, was that informants came out of a small group with specific social and economic characteristics. I tried to solve this problem by continually searching for informants beyond these circles.

Another problem of this method was that it did not allow for a quantitative comparison of workers who were employed in different types of industrial enterprises. There was simply not enough time available to me to track down the number of workers who would have been needed for such an exercise. So I was obliged, though in a later stage, to proceed company by company, rather than through personal contacts.

According to the methodological prerequisites for such a comparison, I had to make a representative selection of industrial units according to such variables as size and technology. This was not possible, since my choice of companies was largely limited to those owners who were on cordial terms with me. Some of them reacted to my requests with the observation, "I will allow this because we are friends; nobody else would tolerate it." There were several selected enterprises whose owners I did not know. I could solve this problem by taking them by surprise, as I did in the case of counting the workers. Some owners, indeed, told me that I was not welcome, while in a few cases I was lucky because they were absent. All in all, I succeeded in collecting data about 185 workers employed in eleven different types of industrial enterprises.

These eleven represented the most important types of industrial enterprises in the research area. However, the problem of representation was not the only obstacle in the way of my attempt to build up a quantitative picture. For instance, I was not able to fully carry out the surveys in the companies. In some cases, the information gathered by this technique was doubtful, especially when the owner was present during its administration. One of the owners even made it a point to act as an interpreter, though I did not require one. Consequently, when it came to asking about working conditions, I was obliged to limit my questions to the most uncontroversial topics. The result was a quantitative picture which was of limited reliability as far as accuracy and completeness were concerned. However, this did not constitute sufficient reason to discard the material, as it offered one of the few possibilities for getting insight into the relevance and size of the phenomena under study.

> I was able, for example, to get some idea about the wages of industrial workers in the area. From the surveys of the 11 enterprises, it appeared that half of the 185 workers received less than Rs. 4 per day, which is very little. From the survey, it also appeared that 50 per cent of the workers owned a piece of land, which in turn had important consequences for the relations which the workers maintained with each other. This percentage was much higher than what I had expected on the basis of the qualitative material which I had collected.

Qualitative Research

By qualitative research, I refer to the technique of soliciting information through rather long, loosely structured interviews. Though I conducted these conversations with a view towards soliciting answers to already formulated questions, it was not my intention to go through all of the topics in one sitting. Often, some questions were exhaustively discussed while others were not raised. Thus, one informant spoke at length about his work history, another about his working conditions and a third about a strike which had failed. The information thus assembled served as a point of departure for further conversations with the same informant, or was used to initiate talks with others. In this way, I was able to exercise some control over the accuracy and the relevance of the information.

> One of the most revealing findings of my study was the antagonism between workers who owned some agrcultural land of their own and those who did not. I discovered it while talking with workers belonging to one family without land who were employed in different industrial firms. This topic was then raised repeatedly in later conversations with others. Almost all the informants appeared to have some opinion on the subject. They admitted the distinction and spoke about the consequences it had with reference to contemplated industrial action. Again, this aspect was further worked out in later conversations with other informants.
> The reconstruction of these industrial actions was based on information obtained from the parties involved. I usually began with very little information, which was developed by trade union leaders, workers, entrepreneurs, labour officers, and well-informed 'outsiders' in a retrospective manner. In this way, I was able to form a reasonably complete picture of the development of strikes and the reasons why they had failed.

Such a fieldwork procedure is based on improvisation, is time-consuming and its course is hard to predict. Its cautious nature lends itself particularly well to studying a field to which there is no easy access. Because it is difficult to anticipate what will be possible and what will not, research strategies often have to be worked out in the field itself. It may even be necessary to modify the research question, or to approach the problem from a different angle from the one which the fieldworker had in mind originally.

Indirect Ways

> Earlier I explained the difficulty of gathering financial data in order to assess the viability of small-scale industrial enterprises. Nevertheless, I wanted to know about the nature and continuity of the investment of capital into industrial

production. To answer this question I changed my perspective to be able to approach the problem in a qualitative manner. The careers of those who invested in industrial production became one of my topics. The respondents did not perceive any threat in this question; on the contrary, they enjoyed talking about it. From their replies, it was possible to deduce that the pattern of investments had been discontinuous and spread out over a variety of commercial and industrial enterprises at the same time.

This example shows how information about continuity of industrial investments can be arrived at in an indirect manner. Research into important aspects of labour relations was conducted in a similar way. The reconstruction of life histories was an important guideline in the study of workers as well. The method provides the unstructured qualitative method with a systematic base. The histories allowed me to initiate conversations and to collect general background information. The approach appeared particulary productive when the careers of the workers were discussed; for instance, how they had found their jobs. The way in which labour is recruited offers the owners the means to control workers. Thus I could gather information about the delicate issue of labour relations. Because I sought these insights through talks which apparently were not threatening to them, workers were willing to reveal details of the relations between themselves and the owners, and among themselves, which they probably would not have disclosed otherwise.

> The informants referred from time to time to colleagues who were in league with the bosses and who were used by them to keep the workers in line. Further, they were able to clarify the reasons for the bonds between these colleagues and the owners.

Apart from patience and flexibility, qualitative research requires that the researcher takes his informants seriously and that he approaches them without preconceived opinions. This is not easy. Contradictions and relations of power set the stage and pace of my fieldwork. I was unable to withdraw from these, even at the level of ideas. The majority of the workers were tribals and untouchables, who carry out the least-valued work in the town and in the countryside. They are very poor, and their ritual and social status is low. Entrepreneurs, government officials and others who belonged to the local elite saw them as 'backwards', as ignorant, untrustworthy and given to drink. They took pains to impress upon me that this view of the workers was true. Because I spent time among the well-to-do and was often dependent on them for care and shelter, the danger that I would be consciously or unconsciously influenced by these prejudices was great. Furthermore, I belong to a society which has its own status and class inequalities, as well as stereotypes about capacities and life styles of subaltern groups; I am prejudiced myself. As a trained sociologist and anthropologist, I was conscious of carrying these views with me while doing fieldwork. Though I tried to suppress them, they seemed to be confirmed sometimes when, indeed, workers did not give accurate information or appeared to be ignorant. Thus I came across workers who did not know whether they received a bonus or paid leaves. This became evident, for instance, during surveys in selected enterprises. When present, the owner took his chance to establish triumphantly that they proved that he really was the only person with whom I should talk about such matters.

Yet 'ignorance' constitutes important information. In this case, it means that the workers were never told about their rights to bonuses or free days, and probably that the workers never received such benefits. It was in the interests of the owners to keep the workers uninformed in order to maintain their control over them.

The ignorance of the workers marks their vulnerable and inferior social position. It did not, however, mean that they were unreliable informants when topics were discussed about which they were able and willing to talk, such as the ways they were treated by the owners, officials, and union leaders; their living and working conditions; and their relationships with each other. In any case, their information was as accurate as that provided by their employers and others who appeared to have 'something to hide'.

Conclusion

This essay dealt with the limited freedom and independence of the researcher during fieldwork. These limitations are at their sharpest when vested interests are at stake and the groups under study relate to each other through dominance and subordination. Gaining access to such a research area is not easy, and the official sources of information are highly incomplete and unreliable. Fieldwork, then, entails a considerable amount of improvisation and continuous adjustment to circumstances, as well as periodically requiring that a blind eye be turned to methodological considerations, and often taking the risk of violating local codes of courtesy. The manner in which I admitted myself to shop floors and took business owners by surprise are examples of the latter.

I am of the opinion that only a combination of quantitative and qualitative techniques can produce a reasonably accurate reconstruction of 'reality'. The research topic and accessibility of the field determine which techniques will dominate. When access is difficult, quantitative research techniques will necessarily suffer from serious shortcomings. The plausibility of the results and insights can hardly be based on figures and statistical techniques.

Instead, the researcher can only produce a satisfactory reconstruction of reality when he uses material collected by more than one technique, gathered from different angles, obtained from different types of informants, and when he continuously cross-checks the information he has assembled.

The problem of having access to the field is also of importance in the implementation of aid programmes. At present (1977) Dutch government and international organisations, like the International Labour Organisation, want such programmes to be aimed directly at the poorest and weakest sections of the populations in the Third World. The problems faced by those who must implement such programmes will be similar to those described above. The informants of the fieldworker form the target group of the development expert. Poverty is part of social and economic subordination and marginality. Efforts to change this are even more threatening to the local elite than the work of the researcher; the local elite will try to thwart such changes and may even threaten the program personnel. Furthermore, it wouldn't be surprising if local elites tried to take control of the new opportunities which open up as a result of these efforts.

The difficulties I faced in approaching the workers in small-scale industries without interference from the owners arose from the workers' 'invisibility'. It must be realised that it is precisely the poorest, especially in South Asia, who are difficult to approach because they are badly organised.

> The trade union leaders who were active among the workers did not consider the representation of the workers' interests as their first priority. Their behaviour was characterised by opportunism and by placing their own interests first. The few times when their intervention was successful, it meant favouring a few; that is, those workers who were under the aegis of the labour laws. In smaller companies not subject to the Factories Act, their presence was disadvantageous. The owners were able to break up the few strike actions which occurred with repression. For example, they threatened to fire those workers who were active and members of the union.

It is almost unavoidable that the implementation of the present development policy, which will be difficult anyhow, will result in a selective approach. Aid will be provided when some efficiency is guaranteed; thus it will be directed towards people who are accessible through organisations. This also means that support does not imply far-reaching political consequences. I am not sure that such aid will necessarily help the poorest or the weakest.

4. *An Amsterdammer in Bulsar*[11]

I went back to Bulsar in 1990 after almost twenty years. My experience there in the early seventies had been so stimulating that it left an indelible mark on my personal life and academic career. Thus, my return was more than just a routine visit; it was like meeting a former beloved. I knew we both had changed and I was not sure whether we would recognize each other, and if she still meant the same to me.

The rendezvous was not disappointing; in fact, our reunion inspired me once again. Despite radical changes, the town and its inhabitants as well as the ambience had remained recognizable, while I realized that I perceived 'reality' differently than I did twenty years ago. With this changed perspective I looked at the overall situation and, more specifically, at the industries in the area[12], as I had done twenty years earlier. The industrial development surprised me and surpassed my expectations.

In this article I will clarify the discrepancy between the situation in 1990 and what I had anticipated. First I will summarize the conlusion I drew in the 1970s. Next I will describe general changes that occurred during the 1980s and the history of one of the entrepreneurs whom I had met in 1971, whose story seems to me to reveal important changes. Then I will explain how my perception in the 1970s did not allow me to make a proper judgement of the industrial development during that period and later on. Finally I will discuss whether my reappraisal of the industrial transition has been forced by the actual situation, or by my changed perspective.

The Conclusion Then

"The results of the development of Bulsar's small industry are hardly encouraging [...] the development which grew primarily out of trade after 1960 is characterized by commercialism, the tendency to set up, successively or simultaneously, diverse commercial activities [...] Commercialism has often been defined as an aspect of the transition to industrial capitalism from merchant capital. That can mean that commercialism is reducible to the business tradition of the new industrialists who are accustomed to easy profits on a short term. Undoubtly this orientation will not be without influence. But this is not a conclusive explanation, because diversity in, and the spreading of, investment also occur among artisan entrepreneurs whose background might suggest otherwise [...] Commercialism is thus not a characteristic of a special social group but inherent in the Indian socio-economic structure. In the first place, the extent of access to the government and community largely determines who is going to become involved in industrial production. Through these contacts, investments in small-scale industry become possible and attractive, and they also allow entrepreneurs to profit from other lucrative possibilities. They can spread their risks, help close kin and others, and make timely reinvestments if profits decrease [...] Despite their contacts, for many small-scale industrialists, long-term entrepreneurship is uncertain. The overall economic structure encourages rather than prevents diverse investments and the spreading of risks. They - the owners of small industrial enterprises - cannot count on a regular supply of reasonably priced raw materials or on a constantly expanding market; after a short time a new and initially lucrative branch of industry is overcrowded. Betting on several horses is a rational entrepreneurial behaviour" (Streefkerk 1985: 258, 259).

I based this conclusion on the research I carried out among industrial entrepreneurs in Bulsar in 1971.[13] They included *Suthars,* craftsmen; *Anavil Brahmins,* the traditional landowning caste of this area; and *Vaisnava* and *Jain Banias,* the merchants and businessmen. Commercialism was prevalent among most of them and it was most clearly manifested by the Jains. They owned the largest number (21 per cent) of the 143 small industrial enterprises in the research area. In 'Jains, Plastics and Stationery' (Streefkerk 1985: 156-162) I discussed their style of entrepreneurship, which I will summarise below.

In 1971, six Jains manufactured plastic items such as switches, containers, buckets, stationery, and small metal appliances in six separate firms. Five of the six firms used more or less identical hand presses employing electrically-heated molds in which plastic or metal raw material is pressed in order to produce the required shape. In terms of technology and product these firms display a significant degree of cohesion. This stems from the close interrelations among the owners of the six firms. They are from the same native area in Kutch, northwest Gujarat. Their grandfathers, who were merchants and money-lenders, lived in villages within 25 kilometers of each other. Their fathers migrated to Bombay, where they became grocers, owners of a stationary store, sold hardware, and invested in building construction. Their sons came to Bulsar, where they opened the industrial workshops.

'Sword Electricals' is the largest of these six firms. It is one of the larger units in the research area as well. The yearly turnover amounts to a few million rupees and there are about 60 workers. Electrical switches are the main product. The firm is owned by Shah, alias Switchwalla, and his family. They started manufacturing switches in Bombay seven years earlier. The desire to broaden the family's economic base made them decide to go into industrial production. Contacts with a switch manufacturer gave Switchwalla the idea of entering this branch, which seemed 'easy and profitable'. At the same time they opened a stationery store and began the production of fountain pens, without success. After all, "we are investors", as he put it. Or, "we are not industrialists; we simply buy the machines and try to sell the plastic buckets", as another owner of one of the six Jain firms confided.[14]

Because small-scale industrialisation in Bulsar was still in its infancy in 1971, I found it difficult to predict in detail its future course. But I was not very optimistic. My idea was that, certainly in the initial stage when regular supply of raw material is uncertain and markets are imperfect, the spreading of risks and commercialism indeed facilitate industrial investments. These require strategic contacts and sufficient capital, which are available only in a few selected groups. Access to these means of production, however, also enables investors to redirect their pursuit of gains as soon as industrial profits decrease or when lucrative industrial enterprises are thwarted otherwise. The result would be industrialization without much continuity.

Bulsar in 1990

There were several reasons for my seven weeks' stay in Bulsar in 1990.[15] One of them was curiosity; I wanted to know whether my earlier characterization of entrepreneurship and evaluation of small-scale industrial development were warranted. I knew from the start that I could not research this issue thoroughly and had to be content with some general impressions and perhaps a few cases. I did not expect that even this limited information would be sufficient to question my earlier conclusions. My doubts were aroused, in part, by the following general tendencies.

First of all, I was surprised by the unexpected sight of Bulsar and its vicinity. Its skyline had changed drastically, with many new flats, numerous TV antennas, and eight multi-storied buildings - each with 10 to 12 stories - built after 1985. The main streets in the centre are overcrowded with cars, scooters, motors and scooter-rickshaws, annoying pedestrians. In the centre, new markets and shopping centres have filled up former open spaces or replaced old buildings. The Kantibhai Desai cricket stadium and sports complex, named after a prominent Anavil who took the initiative to build them, occupy an area which was a large open marshy pond in the heart of the town. The outskirts of the town look different too. Along the roads leading out of the town, residential quarters have come up. For instance, the first part of the erstwhile quiet road to the seaside village of Tithal has become the site of opulent bungalows, luxurious stores, small restaurants, government quarters and air-conditioned offices of businessmen. The largest slum area of Bulsar is called Shapurji Nagar. It is in the reclaimed Dhobi Talav on another edge of the town. To the inhabitants of the neighboring housing societies, the slum-dwellers are a permanent 'threat'. They believe that these people are criminals who are not allowed to live within the limits of the municipal area. Actually, the area is populated by labourers, servants, peons and sweepers, rickshaw drivers, migrants from UP or Kerala, and by families who were forced to vacate their hutments in order to allow the contractors to build new houses. The area also has lepers in the fringe; they have been there for more than 20 years.

To the south of the town, along the river Vanki, 'Vashier Valley' is under construction. This is a residential area on the banks of the river where 85 bungalows are to be built. The project has been undertaken by the two biggest estate developers of Bulsar. The sales prospectus pompously announces that it will be fully equipped with infrastructural facilities such as water supply, street lights and roads, and that there will be a "beautiful children's park and a riverside hide-out for all age groups." The prospectus finally points to the "famous Tithal beach, the site for lovers of sun and surf." It refers to Western sun-bathing and surfing, though generally Indians do not sun-bathe or surf.

The town's population expanded enormously during the last decade, increasing by more than the average growth rate in Gujarat and India. The growth has been caused by both natural increase and immigration: Bulsar became more and more attractive to outsiders. They are mainly from Bombay, and to a lesser extent also from Surat, the fast-growing industrial and commercial city 70 kilometers north of Bulsar. Labour is cheap and the prices of land and houses are still low compared to those in cities like Bombay, Surat or Baroda. Furthermore, life in Bulsar is more comfortable and convenient. It is a small, pleasant town near the sea and can be reached easily by train. Houses and flats are bought as permanent residences or as second homes. The latter is the case in the village of Tithal, where many new flats are owned by Jains from Bombay. Most of the time the buildings are empty, except during some weekends and summer holidays. Bulsar's administrative importance also has brought people to the town. It is a district headquarters with a growing number of offices and civil servants.

There has been rapid growth in all kinds of commercial and professional services and activities. Compared to 1974, there are, for instance, many more medical doctors and private hospitals offering specialized services. Another visible change in the town's life is in the proliferation of scooter-rickshaws. Though they certainly quicken public transport within and outside the town, they are far from convenient because the roads are bumpy and the springs are bad. Their exhaust fumes and noise and their drivers' unpredictable behaviour are a permanent annoyance, even to local people. The latest novelty is to have the vehicle equipped with a cassette player and loudspeakers on both sides of the passengers' seat, like earphones. As soon as the driver turns the ignition key, film music almost blows the passenger out of his seat.

> Rickshaws replaced the Muslim-owned horse-carts, which were the main means of public transport till 1976. Since 1975 the purchase of a rickshaw is facilitated by special bank loans. Many rickshaws are given on rent by the owners to drivers. Among the owners Muslims and *Tandels* (fishermen) predominate. The Tandels live outside Bulsar in coastal villages like Kosamba. They earned money by carrying in their boats goods smuggled from the Arabian coast into India. Some of the other proprietors are government servants or employees of large private industrial firms. Officially their wives or relatives own the three-wheelers. The drivers are Muslims, Tandels, *Kolis* and *Dhodyias*. Several of them are graduates and a few even have a master's degree. Driving a three-wheeler is often a part-time activity, combined with another job.

Because the official records are far from reliable, it was difficult to trace the exact number of three-wheelers in Bulsar. The files of the self-appointed chairman of the 'Bulsar Town Autorikshaw Association' are perhaps the best source. Around 1970 he was one of the first to own and drive a scooter-rickshaw in Bulsar. At present he runs a shop selling scooter-rickshaw spares at the main rickshaw-stand near the bus station. His books show the impressive number of 2860 rickshaws in Bulsar and adjoining villages in 1990. It is hard to believe that so many three-wheelers circulate on the roads of the town and nearby villages. Several rickshaw owners and drivers, however, mentioned the same number when asked for the number of rickshaws in the area. Even though the figures may not be correct, they do indicate a trend. When the self-evident sharp proportional increase in rickshaws in the early seventies is left out of consideration, then the largest increase in number of rickshaws is between 1985 and 1990. In those five years the number of vehicles increased from 1186 to 2862, or by 141 per cent, while between 1980 and 1985 the increase was 116 per cent. Their sharp increase after 1985 parallels the town's expansion in those years. The growing number of rickshaws during the last ten years means that more and more people in Bulsar are willing and able to pay at least two to three rupees, the minimum fare, to be driven from one place to another. It also indicates the emergence of a new transport culture, which means that riders prefer to travel even short distances by mechanical means for reasons of prestige.

The emergence of a middle class[16] is one of the most striking developments of the last ten years. It is a major feature of the class structure of

30

Bulsar in 1990. This middle class is made up of managers, professionals, small-scale industrialists, small businessmen, shop owners, government personnel, employees of private firms, etc. They populate the multi-storied buildings, new flats and residential quarters, and they patronize the fashionable stores in the new shopping centres. They purchase goods made available through the liberalization of the economy in the 1980s, like motorcycles, scooters, cars, refrigerators, televisions and other consumer electronics (ODI 1989: 1, 2).

Changes in the distribution of power accompany the rise of the middle class. For instance, the composition of the municipal council in 1990 shows a much larger proportion of 'middle groups', like *Prajapati*, *Rana* and *Ganchi*, than in 1971. In 1971 these groups occupied 8 per cent of the seats (Thakore 1979: 291); in 1990 the percentage was 31! In 1971, Anavils, Banias and *Parsis* occupied the majority of seats in the council. The largest single group of seats belonged to Parsis, and the mayor was a Parsi (Thakore 1979: 300). In 1990, these groups lost their numerical prominence, though a Parsi is still the council chairman. The Rotary Club, the pre-eminently elite organization of the town, is also no longer dominated by Anavils and Banias. In 1990 representatives of middle-groups, such as Prajapati and Suthar, are members of the Club's executive committee.

Industrial development has been considerable. Many newcomers from Bombay are owners or managers of enterprises which have been brought to South Gujarat in recent years.[17] They are located mostly in the huge GIDC (Gujarat Industrial Development Corporation) industrial estate at Vapi, 25 kilometers south of Bulsar towards the Maharashtra-Gujarat border.[18] At present there are almost 2000 establishments, which is ten times the number in 1970, when the estate was still under construction. The estate is meant primarily for chemical industries. Due to serious air and water pollution and inadequate facilities in the small town of Vapi, owners and managers prefer to stay in Bulsar. In the immediate vicinity of Bulsar, along the national highway and the two state highways, many small-scale and medium-sized industries have come into existence during the last decade as well.

The number of establishments in the Gundlav GIDC industrial estate along one of these roads, 3 kilometers east of Bulsar, had increased as well. After 1985 the estate was extended to the other side of the road. In 1990 the old and new part together accommodated 183 units; in 1971 there were only sixteen enterprises.

Gundlav and Switchwalla in 1990

Many of the 143 firms which in the early 1970s were spread over the town and its vicinity had disappeared. Suthars closed their bobbin factories (Streefkerk 1991) and many units owned by Anavils, Banias and others too had vanished. Of the sixteen establishments which were started at the nearby Gundlav industrial estate in the same period, only four were still present in 1990; nine had disappeared and three had been bogus firms.

The closure of factories by itself is not a sufficient proof of the validity of my idea that commercialism leads to unstable industrial development. The questions are whether these enterprises are part of a series of successive or simultaneous business activities, and what are the reasons for the closures. To answer these questions I concentrated on the Gundlav industrial estate. The tracing of closed enterprises and their owners outside the estate would have taken too much time. One of the 'survivors' in Gundlav helped me with the reconstruction. His general information and my knowledge about industries at Gundlav and their owners in the early 1970s hardly differed.[19]

At least seven of these nine industrial firms which had closed down were not part of other industrial or commercial activities. These industrial firms at Gundlav were the only source of income for their owners. They failed due to a combination of technological, financial, commercial and personal reasons. One of them died without offspring, another was probably murdered. (In 1971 there was a rumour that this man was involved in a family conflict which posed serious problems for the factory.) The other owners left Bulsar; one of them emigrated to Canada.

The eighth enterprise, part of a larger concern, was first sold and then closed because, according to my informant, the new owners were not really interested and managed the firm badly. The ninth factory was a daughter concern of an enterprise in Bombay. Labour troubles made the owners decide to close the factory. Of the four enterprises that still existed in 1990, two were part of commercial and industrial undertakings based in Bombay.

The majority of the factories established in the early seventies at Gundlav collapsed because the owners failed as entrepreneurs. My informant who, like the others, faced serious difficulties in the beginning, phrased these failures as follows: "Here - at Gundlav and in India - many starting industrialists have fancy ideas, but they lack practicality [...] Some made the mistake of developing their own machines, which took time and money without making sufficient income, while a few years later they could have imported or bought these machines."

The last and most important reason why I began to doubt my original judgement of entrepreneurship and industrialization is the surprising history of Switchwalla and his family, owners of 'Sword Electricals' mentioned above.

The family concern expanded between 1971 and 1990 to become the largest producer of plastic switches and allied products in India. This assortment of products includes hundreds of different articles such as numerous types of switches, light dimmers, fan regulators, circuit breakers, and fuse links, as well as musical doorbells. A few years earlier, electric irons, bulbs and tubes were added to this range of products. Furthermore, recently, one of the sons began to manufacture cosmetics. At present, the concern consists of numerous small factories spread across South Gujarat. Some of these are established in towns such as Bulsar, Bilimora, and Navsari, while others are located in the countryside. Tubes and bulbs are manufactured in Madras and Hydrabad. The family became major share-holders of these factories in 1985, and since then the products have been sold under the 'Sword' brand name.

I am not sure about the precise number of undertakings: Switchwalla[20] cited 20, while his sons said they owned 40 to 45 units. These differences in number can apparently be explained by differences in ownership. Many of these enterprises are 'officially' owned not by the family but by the managers of the units, so as to avoid tax and labour laws. According to Switchwalla, numerous small firms are easier to manage then a few large ones. He claims that his success is due to the quality of his products, good advertising and competitive prices.

The production process in most of the units is still based primarily on hand presses and manual labour; it is labour-intensive, not complicated, and thus cheap. According to the management, the concern employs a total of 5000 workers, but I think the actual number of workers is higher. Most of the workers are women, both young and old. The explanation offered in the head office in Bombay and by some managers in Bulsar is that women are best suited for the delicate handwork required for the job. Furthermore, women are cheaper than men and the labour turnover among them is less because "the Indian woman is strongly tied to the house." Moreover, it is often said, probably not without reason, that girls and women from the villages like to work in the factories because they can contribute to the incomes of their households without having to work in the fields, which is much heavier work, offers less freedom and often pays less.

I visited a few Sword units in Bulsar. One employed 8 men and 100 women who all assembled switch parts. Another was an engineering workshop which employed not more than 9 persons, so that it would not come under the purview of the Factories Act. Copper parts of switches were made with the help of powered presses. According to the supervisor of the large unit some of the workers were employed permanently and others as 'helpers'. Permanent workers have rights to bonus, paid leave and provident fund. Their wage is Rs 17 or Rs 18 per day (in 1990 the official minimum wage was Rs 21). They sometimes earn more (Rs 20 to Rs 25) because their wage is supplemented by piece rate. 'Helpers' are temporary workers, they earn less and are not eligible for the above-mentioned facilities. The factories run 6 days a week for nine hours a day. Unlike other factories at Gundlav there are no night-shifts so that women do not have to travel after dark.

Since I did not have the opportunity to compare this information with what the women themselves said about the conditions of their work, it must be handled with caution. In any case, the factories looked neat and tidy. Further, the women had their own toilet facilities and there was a row of fifteen taps to wash themselves and keep their tiffin boxes clean. Moreover, clothed colorfully, they evoked a cheerful mood. They came from neighboring villages and were mostly Kolis and tribals like Dhodiyas or *Dublas*.

One of the most remarkable sections of the concern is the great distribution centre just outside Bulsar. The centre is located in the site where Switchwalla and his brother started their small factory in 1968. Around 1980 this unit was shifted to the Gundlav industrial estate to make room for a few sturdy warehouses. All finished and semi-processed products, as well as raw materials from various parts of India, are collected and stored there. The goods are subsequently sent to clients or to units which work on the raw materials or semi-processed products. The transport of these goods is organized by the family itself. More than twenty trucks drive the goods from suppliers to Bulsar, and from Bulsar to factories and clients. There are about 200 employees in the offices and warehouses.

The history of the Switchwalla family and the information about first-generation entrepreneurs at Gundlav are too selective to draw conclusions from. However, the case of Switchwalla together with the general development of Bulsar and its vicinity certainly do provide grounds for me to rethink my opinion of small-scale industrial development.

The closed enterprises at Gundlav show that the first stage of industrial entrepreneurship is a difficult period and that it is problematic to use the facts about this period as evidence for the style of entrepreneurship. The history of the Switchwallas reveals that commercialism does not necessarily lead to an unstable industrial development. The present manner of Switchwalla's entrepreneurship does not seem to differ from earlier descriptions. Even in 1990, business owners claimed that 'horizontal diversification', or what I termed 'betting on different horses', is an important condition for successful entrepreneurship. Open for debate, therefore, is my evaluation[21] of the industrial development which I had based on this type of entrepreneurship. Such a debate could stress the greater weight of ideas in evaluating a phenomenon than in describing it. However, as far as subjectivity is concerned, the difference between evaluation and description is not so clearly marked. Neither does describing a phenomenon happen independently of the views of the researcher.

This fact, the researcher as research instrument, is a characteristic of socio-anthropological fieldwork. The different stages of the research procedure are combined within one person. That's why the gathering of data, analysis and evaluation are highly sensitive to the personality, perception and theories of the fieldworker. Moreover, it appears that the study of small-scale industries lends itself pre-eminently to projections of the ideas of the fieldworker. Sandesara (1988: 644) points out that the small-scale industrial development is susceptible to several interpretations: "One can say almost anything, even statistically, ranging from the most complimentary to the most derogatory, on small industry." My astonishment about Bulsar, and about Switchwalla in particular, requires the reconstruction of my theoretical and methodological perspectives at the commencement of my fieldwork and during the elaboration of my data. It is based on notes, on conversations with those who were involved with my study in the seventies, and earlier publications. I did it before I boarded the plane for Bombay in 1990.

Amsterdam in the Early Seventies

A few months before I left for South Gujarat in 1971, I completed my studies in sociology and cultural anthropology at the University of Amsterdam. They were theoretically informed, research-oriented, bore a structural-functionalist stamp, and offered a historical and comparative perspective as well. Further, some professors taught me to be socially concerned. This tendency became more manifest as my study progressed and both teachers and students showed increased dissatisfaction with structural-functionalism. When I left for India I was familiar with a diverse range of authors and views. My knowledge was derived from general theoretical questions, the sociology and anthropology of India, and of Gujarat in particular.[22] I felt attracted to the political anthropology of writers like Bailey (1969) and Boissevain (1968) who gave patronage, coalitions and networks a central place in their studies. Authors who emphasised culture and religion in their accounts appealed less to me.

The Indo-Dutch project which I joined had as its central theme 'the modernising process in South Gujarat'. Since the study of entrepreneurs in small-scale industries was reserved for me, I consulted mainly American authors.[23] Initially, I was not very charmed by the subject. The presupposed importance of entrepreneurs as a source of change and dynamism seemed to me too 'Western' and the focus on entrepreneurs too limiting. But as my research progressed, my fascination with the subject grew. I was able to steer the fieldwork into an intellectually rewarding direction. How successful entrepreneurs controlled capital, labour, and other means of production became one of my leading questions. Further, I concentrated on reconstructing the industrial history of South Gujarat.

I returned to Amsterdam more socially concerned than I had been when I left in 1971, and I found that anthropology and sociology there appeared to have been drastically radicalised. This radicalization was one of the ideological changes which occurred in that period; artists, for instance, changed their opinions as well. From 1970 onwards, young and talented composers, musicians, and actors undertook actions against "the conservative and capitalist power structures which underlie the politics of art and culture" (Koopmans 1977: 160). The political climate also changed. The ideal of more equal distribution of incomes and power gained importance. The program of the Labour Party, the largest and most moderate of the political parties to advocate this ideal, stressed democratization of education, industrial relations and administration; levelling of incomes; further expansion of the welfare state; and an aid and development policy aimed at the basic needs of the Third World population (Bleich 1986: 139-141). The party won the parliamentary elections in 1973 and it led, for the first time in several years, a centre-left government until 1977.

At the University of Amsterdam, the marxist-inspired political economy of development and underdevelopment had become dominant. The conditions of the poor and their emancipation had become important topics (Wertheim 1974). This meant that research was no longer taken for granted, but had to be 'useful' and serve 'the less-endowed and powerless'. The works of, among others, Alavi (1964, 1972), Baran (1968), Bettelheim (1971), Frank (1969) and Gough and Sharma (1973) were 'eye-openers' for me, and shaped my perspective. This reorientation was further prompted by misgivings that my interest in entrepreneurs was not appreciated by the dominant group of sociologists and anthropologists in Amsterdam[24], and by my wish to be accepted by them. All these led to an anti-capitalist perspective: entrepreneurial production was no solution to India's problems because it would result in half-hearted modernization and ill-balanced progress. Entrepreneurs were an exponent of these developments, and in a certain sense they were the 'bad guys', or 'agents in underdevelopment' (Streefkerk 1979).

The elaboration and analysis of my data were based on the combination of the above-cited perspective and the type of material I had gathered as a social anthropologist. The commercialism of the entrepreneurs and the consequent instability of industrial development were important in my reconstruction of the industrial situation. When I recently looked through my material again after a long gap, I discovered, indeed, that I had not been totally unbiased in my work. For example, I had not paid sufficient attention to a concern which had been based for many years in Bombay and subsequently shifted to Bulsar in 1967. The concern, consisting of eight small metal-based factories and a paint workshop, was flourishing at that time and has continued to do so for the last two decades. Its major product is anodised aluminum plates 'for decoration and practical application', but it also manufactures machine parts and metal toys. A large portion of the shares of the concern, a private limited company, is owned by Jains, originally from Bulsar, who founded the company. The head office is still in Bombay, and there are branch offices in Calcutta and Bhopal.

In short, even in 1971 evidence was already available that commercialism and industrial instability are not necessarily related.

Discussion

The history of Switchwalla and his family and recent developments in Bulsar do not fit in my original discourse on entrepreneurship and industrial development. My initial theoretical preferences and methodology, together with the ideological climate in Amsterdam and the prevailing discussions over development and underdevelopment, excluded processes which occurred in South Gujarat in the last two decades. More specifically, my anti-capitalist perspective offered little room for a more sympathetic evaluation of entrepreneurs and their achievements. This tendency is manifested especially in the taken-for-granted coupling of the style of entrepreneurship with the quality of industrialization. The first can still stand the empirical test. It is suitable in contexts characterized by economic insecurity and an emphasis on social dependability, the capacity to honour obligations to family, relatives and other primordial relationships. Therefore, the conclusion that this style of entrepreneurship necessarily leads to uncertain and unstable industrial development needs further re-examination.

The question that remains to be answered is whether this re-appraisal is based on the 1990 situation alone or on other considerations as well. The 'Bulsar of 1990' has indeed amazed me, but it has not taken me totally by surprise. The expansion of the town, the industrial situation and the history of Switchwalla provided food for doubts which I had harbored already for some time. They arose from a combination of personal experiences, societal events and other academic insights. The first made me, among other things, more aloof and led me to re-consider my ideas. Prevailing academic perspectives also changed. The events in China, Vietnam and Cambodia, for instance, have certainly contributed to these changes. The one-sidedness of the political economy analysis was more clearly recognized, though historical perspectives and the theory of world-wide development of capitalism (Wolf 1982) still persisted. But local conditions, and their cultural specifity in particular, received more attention. At the same time, I was better able to see the participants in the world-wide expansion of capitalism in their contexts and to study them from their own perspectives. This does not mean that I became less critical or emotionally more indifferent. But it does imply a more balanced approach to industrial entrepreneurship; without, however, neglecting the conditions of workers and questions of dominance and subordination. It also meant a greater openness to cultural characteristics of Indian society, such as ideas about hierarchy and caste.

The problem of 'restudy and different results' is part of modern anthropology based on fieldwork. Redfield's Tepoztlan differed from the Tepoztlan described by Lewis, and Samoan social reality presented by Freeman deviated from that described earlier by Mead. Kloos deals extensively with the different outcomes of research conducted by different fieldworkers who studied the same society or the same group of people at different moments. He offers several explanations for the discrepancy between earlier and later results. One is the fact that, indeed, changes have occurred during the period between the first and second study. The other refers to different interpretations based on explicit theoretical preferences of the researchers. Such a theoretical preference, ultimately, arises from an implicit ideological perspective which, in turn, is related to the social background of the fieldworker (1988: 120-122). I agree with Kloos' analysis, though my experiences in Bulsar are more complicated. First, the two possibilities just mentioned have to be combined: The situation changed and so did the perspective from which it was viewed. Second, these different perceptions do not belong to two different fieldworkers but reflect changes within one person.

Literature on the question of 're-exposure' and changed perspectives of fieldworkers is scarce. One would expect that the subject is dealt with in literature on long-term field research such as the volume compiled by Foster, Scudder, Colson and Kemper (1979). In this book the problem of assessing the value of anthropological data which reflects the interests and perspectives of young people in their twenties and early thirties is indeed noticed. Several contributors (Meggitt 1979: 112; Scudder and Colson 1979: 251) point to the question of the aging anthropologist. But the awareness does not seem to go beyond the acceptance of the former graduate student following a trajectory 'from whippersnapper to elder', and reaping the benefits therefrom. The aging anthropologist certainly "reevaluates field records collected at a younger age, but equally there is no doubt that what seems to be significant or what can be learned is different at different periods" (Foster et al. 1979: 331).

The question of changed perspectives seems to apply only to those who have been investigated, like the Mexican people who were studied by Foster in the forties and fifties. He acknowledges that if he had begun his research later, say in 1970, the idea of 'limited good' probably never would have occurred to him. A young anthropologist could certainly argue, on the basis of findings collected today, that the hypothesis of 'limited good' would no longer be appropriate. "World views can and do change" (Foster 1979: 176), but obviously not those of the fieldworker. One might wonder why the problem of changed perspectives and long-term fieldwork has not been raised in the book. A tentative answer could be that the authors were not fully aware of the social origin of the production of knowledge, or not yet prepared to accept the idea.

5. *Postscript*

My experiences in South Gujarat reveal how procedures and ideology modify the production of knowledge based on fieldwork. Procedures include the types of interaction between informants and fieldworker and the improvisational nature of fieldwork. The ideology of the researcher is a second ingredient in the creation of knowledge. By ideology I mean the fieldworker's frame of reference, reflecting the general social background, the values of the academic reference group, and the theoretical perspective of the researcher. Procedures and ideology do not exist independently. They are combined within one person and, moreover, procedures are subordinated to ideological considerations; they tend to determine research procedures. Thus, the positivistic natural science ideal stresses a strict methodological format to be able to count, measure and perform statistical operations. The critique of this ideal has been attended by a wider use and recognition of qualitative methods.

Research procedures are instrumental in the production of knowledge. However, their role is of a technical kind. Ideological considerations play a far more directing, compelling, or, if one likes, dramatic part in the fieldworker's creation. They determine the selection of problems and the interpretation of information gathered. They cause divergent representations and valuations of the same processes and phenomena by different researchers, or different interpretations of the same subject by the same fieldworker over the years.

My tentative reappraisal of entrepreneurship in Bulsar in 1991 is an example of the latter. It does raise the problem of the credibility of the different interpretations; in other words, which explanation is more believable, the recent one or the one I presented earlier. I cannot answer this question unambiguously because I am aware, much more than in the seventies, that my latest interpretation is coloured by my frame of reference. Unfortunately, I am unable to be very specific about my present perspective because such a reconstruction can be made only after a longer period of time. Nevertheless, I do realize that my rethinking of entrepreneurship coincides, for instance, with the diminished glamour of marxism in academic circles, with debates on the necessity to contain the role of the welfare state, and with a general tendency to venerate private enterprise and free play of market forces.

Furthermore, after two decades I am still of the opinion that the credibility of the fieldworker's creation is determined by whether or not it is supported by cultural characteristics and facts of material life. The first pertain to, amongst others, religious convictions and ideas about hierarchy, caste, family and kinship. The second include variables such as population numbers, the distribution of landed property and of income, rural and urban wage levels, size of the industrial labour force, or the number of small-scale factories. The second type of variables provided the grounds for me to rethink my opinion of entrepreneurship in Bulsar.

Ultimately readers decide which interpretation is the most or least convincing. It is the task of the fieldworker to provide the information that enables them to reach this conclusion.

Notes

1. Henceforth I will use terms like small-scale enterprises, firms, units and establishments as synonyms.
2. The research tradition in South Gujarat has a comparatively long history. For more than thirty years, the area has been studied intensively by Indian scholars and, above all, by Dutch sociologists and anthropologists. In the early 1960s, four of the latter - Baks, Breman, Hommes and van der Veen - carried out fieldwork in rural areas of South Gujarat. Later they shifted their perspective from the 'local' to the 'regional' level. Between 1970 and 1972 a new project was initiated, and a team of Indian and Dutch researchers based in Bulsar carried out fieldwork in South Gujarat. Their work covered a number of fields and themes, and was aimed at tracing and analysing processes of social change in the town and surrounding countryside. The results of this Indo-Dutch research project have been published in Pillai & Baks (1979). Other publications based on this research include Hommes (1971) on Parsis, Schenk-Sandbergen (1975) on the sweepers of Bulsar, Van der Veen (1976) on the joint family, Breman (1985) on migration and rural labour and Streefkerk (1985) on industrial transition in the region.
3. This discussion was largely inspired by the previous involvement of anthropologists in the preparation and implementation of colonial policy, and by their participation - often unwilling - in counterinsurgency research in Latin America and Southeast Asia after the Second World War.
4. In the United States this led to debates related to the Ethics Committee's reports in the AAA *Newsletters* and the 'Social Responsibility Symposia' in *Current Anthropology* (Scholte 1972: 430).
5. It is typical that the official organisation which provided money for the translation of Van der Veen's dissertation (1969) initially refused to finance the chapter in which he wrote about his fieldwork in a way which was unconventional at the time.
6. Clifford (1986: 14) writes that during this period "a sub-genre of ethnographic writing emerged, the self-reflexive 'fieldwork' account [...] Ethnographic experience and the participant-observation ideal [were] shown to be problematic."
7. The inclusion of ideas in textbooks is a measure of their acceptance. The textbook written by the Keesings, which has served as a first introduction to the discipline for many generations of anthropologists, and which is still widely used as an introductory text, is illustrative. In his early work, Keesing senior (1958, 1964) did not devote any attention to philosophy of science issues. This did happen when his son became co-author. In the 1971 edition they point out that the anthropologist "must organize his knowledge in terms of an existing design and interpret new experiences in terms of familiar ones [...] [which] distorts his perceptions" (Felix & Roger Keesing 1971: 13). In a

later edition of the book, (1976: 6) Roger Keesing writes that "our cultural values (for example prudiness) and psychological orientations predispose us to see and record selectively." A few years later (1981: 6) he states that "in the case of anthropology [the methods] are shaped very directly by the nature of the encounters in which anthropologists observe and learn."
Hastrup & Ovesen (1983: 48) assume in their textbook that the personal situation and point of view of the anthropologist influence his or her work and that criteria of objectivity which are applied in the natural sciences cannot be simply adopted in the social sciences.

8. For a number of decades the relations of production in the cities and the countryside in South and Southeast Asia, both contemporary and historical, has been an important research topic in the South and Southeast Asian section of the Anthropology Department of the University of Amsterdam.

9. Only Rutten (1991: 48) points to the unreliability of his quantitative data.

10. In the sixties many industrial enterpreneurs moved their firms from Bombay to Bulsar. One of the reasons to settle in Bulsar was the labour unrest in Bombay and the quiet conditions in South Gujarat.

11. I thank Arni Hubbeling and Klaas van der Veen, who encouraged me to write on this theme.

12. A follow-up study of my earlier research on the industrial development of that area has been carried out by Pieter Gorter, a Ph.D. student at the University of Amsterdam.

13. My conclusions are discussed by Holmström (1985: 91ff).

14. The story of Papu, the Jain stockbroker from Bombay, in Naipaul's latest book on India (1990: 11) shows that, despite much evidence to the contrary, the idea that Jains are not suitable for industrial entrepreneurship is still alive. He says, "We are traders [...] The killer instinct is required in industry, not in trading. Which is why the Jain community is not involved in industry. If I'm trading in the stock exchange now, and I cannot get some money from the guy, I wouldn't hire a mafia guy to get it out of him. Which is what happens here in something like the building industry [...]"

15. See Streefkerk (1991).

16. I use the term in a statistical manner to describe a category of people, a class-in-itself, with roughly the same income and consumer behaviour.

17. The shifting of Bombay enterprises to Gujarat could already be observed in the late sixties and early seventies (Streefkerk 1985: 53).

18. Vapi is the biggest of several industrial townships in the southernmost part of South Gujarat, which developed between 1970 and 1990.

19. The reconstruction of the recent industrial past of the Suthars was much easier because I still had many contacts among them. The downfall of the first generation of Suthars, who began the industrial production of wooden bobbins around 1940, started in the late sixties. This trend continued in the seventies and eighties; due to technical and commercial reasons Suthars had to close their firms. In 1990, a few of them still manufactured wooden products, but their workshops led a marginal existence (Streefkerk 1991).

20. Around 1975, Switchwalla and his family shifted from Bulsar to Bombay. There they reside in the most expensive part of the city, at Malabar Hill. At present Switchwalla is a 'public figure' with many important political friends. For instance, he lobbies for the construction of the controversial Narmada Dam in western India. He hopes that the dam will end the droughts in Kutch, his native place.
21. I do not use the term analysis because of its connotation of 'objectivity'.
22. The authors I studied ranged from Elias (1969) to Wertheim (1964), Levy (1966), and Barrington Moore (1966), and from Weber (1958) to Mayer (1960), Epstein (1962), Srinivas (1962), Beteille (1965), Van der Veen (1969), and Breman (1970).
23. For instance, Geertz (1963) and Hoselitz (1960, 1968).
24. These misgivings were confirmed, for instance, during job interviews at the University of Amsterdam, when members of selection committees spoke conceitedly about my research.

References

Alavi, Hamza
    1964   Imperialism, Old and New. *Socialist Register*, London.
    1972   The State in Post-Colonial Societies. *New Left Review*, No. 74.
Bailey, F.G.
    1969   *Stratagems and Spoils: A Social Anthropology of Politics.* Oxford: Basil Blackwell.
Baran, Paul A.
    1968   *The Political Economy of Growth.* New York: Monthly Review Press.
Barrington Moore
    1966   *Social Origins of Dictatorship and Democracy: Lord and Peasant in the Making of the Modern World.* Boston: Beacon Press.
Barnes, J.A.
    1967   Some Ethical Problems in Modern Fieldwork. In: D.G. Jongmans and P.C.W. Gutkind (eds.), *Anthropologist in the Field.* Assen: Van Gorcum.
Beteille, Andre
    1965   *Caste, Class and Power.* Berkeley: University of California Press.
Bettelheim, Charles
    1971   *India Independent.* New York: Monthly Review Press.
Bleek, Wolf
    1978   *Achter de coulissen van antropologisch veldwerk in Ghana.* Assen: Van Gorcum.
Bleich, Anet
    1986   *Een partij in de tijd: Veertig jaar Partij van de Arbeid.* Amsterdam: De Arbeiderspers.
Boissevain, J.F.
    1968   *Netwerken en quasi groepen: Enkele beschouwingen over de plaats van niet-groepen.* Assen: Van Gorcum.
Breman, J.C.
    1969   *Meester en knecht: Een onderzoek naar de veranderingen in de betrekkingen tussen landheren en landarbeiders in Zuid Gujarat, India.* Universiteit van Amsterdam.
    1985a   Between Accumulation and Immiseration: The Partiality of Fieldwork in Rural India. *The Journal of Peasant Studies*, Vol. 13, No. 1.
    1985b   *Of Peasants, Migrants and Paupers: Rural Labour Circulation and Capitalist Production in West India*, Delhi: Oxford University Press.
Brunt, Lodewijk (ed.)
    1977   *Anders bekeken: Wet en werkelijkheid in sociaal onderzoek.* Meppel: Boom.
Brunt-de Wit, E.
    1972   Cijfers en twijfels in sociologie en antropologie. *Sociologische Gids*, Jrg. 19, No. 1.

Brymer, R.A. and Buford Farris
1967   Ethical and Political Dilemmas in the Investigation of Deviance: A Study of Juvenile Delinquency. In G. Sjoberg (ed.), *Ethics, Politics and Social Research*. Cambridge, Mass.: Schenkman Publishing Company.

Clifford, James
1986   Introduction: Partial Truths. In James Clifford and George E. Marcus, *Writing Culture: The Poetics and Politics of Ethnography*. Delhi: Oxford University Press.

Elias, N.
1939   *Uber den Prozess der Civilization. Soziogenetische und Psychogenetische Untersuchungen*. Erster Band: *Wandlungen des Verhaltens in den Weltlichen Oberschichten des Abendlandes*. Basel: Verlag Haus Zum Falken.

Epstein, T. Scarlett
1962   *Economic Development and Social Change in South India*. Manchester: Manchester University Press.

Evans-Pritchard, E.E.
1964   *Social Anthropology and Other Essays*. New York: The Free Press.

Frank, Andre Gunder
1969   *Latin America, Underdevelopment or Revolution*. New York: Monthly Review Press.

Foster, George M., et al.
1979   *Long-term Field Research in Social Anthropology*. New York: Academic Press.

Foster, George M.
1979   Fieldwork in Tzintzuntzan: The First Thirty Years. In George M. Foster et al., *Long-term Field Research in Social Anthropology*. New York: Academic Press.

Geertz, Clifford
1963   *Peddlers and Princes: Social Change and Economic Modernization*. Chicago: University of Chicago Press.

Gold, R.L.
1969   Roles in Sociological Field Observation. In G.J. McCall and J.L. Simmons (eds.), *Issues in Participant Observation: A Text and Reader*. Reading, Mass.: Addison-Wesley Publishing Company.

Gough, Kathleen and Hari P. Sharma (eds.)
1973   *Imperialism and Revolution in South Asia*. New York: Monthly Review Press.

Hastrup, Kirsten and Jan Ovesen
1983   *Basisboek culturele antropologie*. Groningen: Wolters-Noordhoff.

Herdt, Gilbert and Robert J. Stoller
1990   *Intimate Communications: Erotics and the Study of Culture*. New York: Columbia University Press.

Holmström, Mark
1985   *Industry and Inequality: The Social Anthropology of Indian Labour*. Cambridge: Cambridge University Press.

Hommes, Enno W.
  1971   Parsis in India: Een bedreigde minderheid. In *Buiten de grenzen, sociolo-
          gische opstellen aangeboden aan Prof. dr. W.F. Wertheim*. Meppel:
          Boom.
Hoseliz, Bert F.
  1960   *Sociological Aspects of Economic Growth*. New York: The Free Press.
Hoseliz, Bert F. (ed.)
  1968   *The Role of Small Industry in the Process of Economic Growth*. The
          Hague: Mouton.
Hüsken, Frans
  1988   *Een dorp op Java: Sociale differentiatie in een boerengemeenschap 1859-
          1980*. Overveen: Acasea
Jarvie, I.C.
  1969   The Problem of Ethical Integrity in Participant Observation. *Current
          Anthropology*, Vol. 10, No. 5.
Keesing, Felix M.
  1964   *Cultural Anthropology: The Science of Custom*. New York: Holt, Rine-
          hart and Winston.
Keesing, Roger M. and Felix M. Keesing
  1971   *New Perspectives in Cultural Anthropology*. New York: Holt, Rinehart
          and Winston.
Keesing, Roger M.
  1976   *Cultural Anthropology: A Contemporary Perspective*. New York: Holt,
          Rinehart and Winston.
  1981   *Cultural Anthropology: A Contemporary Perpective*. New York: Holt,
          Rinehart and Winston, second edition.
Köbben, A.J.F.
  1972   Sociale wetenschappen en ethiek. *Sociologische Gids*, Jrg. 19, No. 5-6.
Kloos, P.
  1969   Role Conflicts in Social Field Work. *Human Organization*, Vol. 10,
          No. 5.
  1972   Marginaal. *Sociologische Gids*, Jrg. 19, No. 5-6.
  1987   *Filosofie van de antropologie*. Leiden: Martinus Nijhoff.
  1988   *Door het oog van de antropoloog: Botsende visies bij heronderzoek*.
          Muiderberg: Dick Coutinho.
Koopmans, Rudy
  1977   *Jazz: Improvisatie en organisatie van een groeiende minderheid*. Amster-
          dam: SUA.
Levy, Marion J., Jr.
  1966   *Modernization and the Structure of Societies: A Setting for International
          Affairs*. Princeton: Princeton University Press.
Lundberg, D.D.
  1968   The Transactional Conception of Field Work. *Human Organization*, Vol.
          27, No. 1.

47

Mayer, Adrian C.
1960   *Caste and Kinship in Central India: A Village and its Region.* Berkeley: University of California Press.

Meggitt, M.J.
1979   Reflections Occasioned by Continuing Anthropological Field Research among the Enga of Papua New Guinea. In George M. Foster et al., *Long-term Field Research in Social Anthropology*. New York: Academic Press.

Nadel, S.F.
1939   The Interview Technique in Social Anthropology. In F.C. Bartlett, M. Ginsberg, E.J. Lindgren, R.H. Thouless (eds.), *The Study of Society*. London: Kegan Paul.

Naipaul, V.S.
1990   *India, a Million Mutinies Now*. London: Heinemann.

Nieuwenhuys, Olga
1990   *Angels with Callous Hands: Children's Work in Rural Kerala (India)*. University of Amsterdam, Ph.D. thesis.

Overseas Development Institute
1989   India's Economy after the Elections. Briefing Paper. London: Overseas Development Institute.

Olden, J.F. van
1972   Antropologie en ethiek: Geannoteerde bibliografie. *Sociologische Gids*, Jrg. 19, No. 5-6.

Pillai, S. Devadas & C. Baks
1979   *Winners and Losers: Styles of Development and Change in an Indian Region*. Bombay: Popular Prakashan.

Rutten, Mario
1991   *Capitalist Entrepreneurs and Economic Diversification: Social Profile of Large Farmers and Rural Industrialists in Central Gujarat, India*. University of Amsterdam: Ph.D. thesis.

Rutten, Rosanne
1990   *Artisans and Entrepreneurs in the Rural Philippines: Making a Living and Gaining Wealth in Two Commercialized Crafts*. Amsterdam: VU University Press.

Sandesara, J.C.
1988   Small-scale Industrialization: The Indian Experience. *Economic and Political Weekly*, Vol. XXIII, No. 13.

Schenk-Sandbergen, L.
1975   *Vuil werk, schone toekomst? Het leven van straatvegers en vuilruimers, een onderzoek in Bulsar (India) en verkenningen in Peking, Shanghai, Tientsin en Tangshan (China)*. Amsterdam: Van Gennep.

Schenk-Sandbergen, Loes Ch. and Hans Schenk
1979   The Setting of Polarity: Introduction to the Research Area. In S. Devadas Pillai & C. Baks (eds.), *Winners and Losers: Styles of Development and Change in an Indian Region*. Bombay: Popular Prakashan.

Scholte, Bob
1972   *Toward a Reflexive and Critical Anthropology.* In Dell Hymes (ed.),
        Reinventing Anthropology, New York: Pantheon Books (first published
        1969).
Scudder, Thayer and Elizabeth Colson
1979   Long-term Research in Gwembe Valley, Zambia. In George M. Foster et
        al., *Long-term Field Research in Social Anthropology*. New York: Aca-
        demic Press.
Srinivas, M.N.
1962   *Caste in Modern India and Other Essays.* Bombay: Asia Publishing
        House.
Streefkerk, Hein
1972   Over participeren en manipuleren. *Sociologische Gids*, Jrg. 19, No. 5-6.
1977   Sluip- en omwegen: Onderzoek bij arbeiders en bazen in India. In Lode-
        wijk Brunt (ed.), *Anders bekeken: Wet en werkelijkheid in sociaal onder-
        zoek*. Meppel: Boom.
1979   Small Entrepreneurs: Agents in Underdevelopment? In S. Devadas Pillai
        & C. Baks (eds.), *Winners and Losers: Styles of Development and
        Change in an Indian Region.* Bombay: Popular Prakashan.
1985   *Industrial Transition in Rural India: Artisans, Traders and Tribals in
        South Gujarat.* Bombay: Popular Prakashan.
1991   Transformation in Bulsar: Suthars and the Relevance of Caste. *Economic
        and Political Weekly*, Vol. XXVI, No. 21.
Thakore, G.D.
1979   A Portrait of Municipal Councilors. In S. Devadas Pillai & C. Baks
        (eds.), *Winners and Losers: Styles of Development and Change in an
        Indian Region.* Bombay: Popular Prakashan.
Veen, Klaas W. van der
1969   *Huwelijk en hierarchie bij de Anavil Brahmanen van Zuid Gujarat,
        sociale verandering en ideologische continuiteit in de Indiase samen-
        leving.* Amsterdam: Universiteit van Amsterdam.
1976   The Joint Family: Persistence or Decay. In S. Devadas Pillai (ed.),
        Aspects of Changing India. Studies in Honour of Prof. G.S. Ghurye.
        Bombay: Popular Prakashan.
Weber, Max
1958   *The Religion of India.* Glencoe: The Free Press.
Wersch van, Hub
1989   *Bombay Textile Strike 1982-83: Workers' Views and Strategies.* Univer-
        sity of Amsterdam: Ph.D. thesis.
Wertheim, W.F.
1964   *East-West Parallels: Sociological Approaches to Modern Asia.* The
        Hague: Van Hoeve.
1974   *Evolution and Revolution, the Rising Waves of Emancipation.* Ham-
        mondsworth: Penguin Books Ltd.

Wolf, Eric R.
  1982   *Europe and the People without History.* Berkeley: University of California Press.